TO MY BELOVED

BR

Sh

Wonderful

By Kenneth E. Hagin

MERRY XAMS

Chapter 1
HIS NAME IS WONDERFUL

For unto us a child is born, unto us a son is given: and the government shall be upon his shoulder: and his name shall be called WONDERFUL, Counsellor, The mighty God, The everlasting Father, The Prince of Peace.

— Isaiah 9:6

FROM

DAISY

In this text, Isaiah, by the Spirit of God, is prophesying concerning the birth of Jesus, the coming Messiah.

We could preach a sermon or two on the phrase "his name shall be called Wonderful," then preach several on "Counsellor" and "The mighty God." In fact, we could almost preach forever on these phrases.

Thank God, Jesus is *all* of them and even more! In this message we will consider the phrase "his name shall be called Wonderful."

At Christmastime, we acknowledge the birth of the Lord Jesus Christ. However, if His birth is all there were to it — if He was born and it ended there — there would be no plan of salvation.

Let's look at God's plan from beginning to end:

Certainly He is Wonderful.

Certainly His conception was Wonderful.

His childhood was Wonderful.

He was Wonderful in ministry.

He was Wonderful in His death.

He was Wonderful in His Resurrection.

And, thank God, He's going to be Wonderful in His coming again.

All of this can be seen in connection with the Christmas story. We'll let the Scriptures speak for themselves.

First, He was Wonderful in conception and the announcing of His birth. All of the writers of the Gospel cover the story, but because Luke goes into a little more detail, I like his account best:

LUKE 1:26-37

26 And in the sixth month the angel Gabriel was sent from God unto a city of Galilee, named Nazareth,

27 To a virgin espoused to a man whose name was Joseph, of the house of David; and the virgin's name was Mary.

28 And the angel came in unto her, and said, Hail, thou art highly favoured, the Lord is with thee: blessed art thou among women.

29 And when she saw him, she was troubled at his saying, and cast in her mind what manner of salutation this should be.

30 And the angel said unto her, Fear not, Mary: for thou hast found favour with God.

31 And, behold, thou shalt conceive in thy womb, and bring forth a son, and shalt call his name JESUS.

32 He shall be great, and shall be called the Son of the Highest: and the Lord God shall give unto him the throne of his father David:

33 And he shall reign over the house of David for ever; and of his kingdom there shall be no end.

34 Then said Mary unto the angel, How shall this be, seeing I know not a man?

35 And the angel answered and said unto her, The Holy Ghost shall come upon thee, and the power of the Highest shall overshadow thee: therefore also that holy thing which shall be born of thee shall be called the Son of God.

36 And, behold, thy cousin Elisabeth, she hath also conceived a son in her old age: and this is the sixth month with her, who was called barren.

37 For with God nothing shall be impossible.

The announcement that Jesus was to be born was Wonderful — an angel came down to announce it!

Furthermore, His conception was Wonderful. Mary was questioning how it could be possible that a virgin could conceive and bear a son. The angel replied, *"The Holy Ghost shall come upon thee, and the power of the Highest shall overshadow thee: therefore also that holy thing which shall be born of thee shall be called the Son of God"* (v. 35).

LUKE 1:38-40
38 And Mary said, Behold the handmaid of the Lord; be it unto me according to thy word. And the angel departed from her.
39 And Mary arose in those days, and went into the hill country with haste, into a city of Juda;
40 And entered into the house of Zacharias, and saluted Elisabeth.

As Luke notes in chapter 2, Mary didn't tell anybody about the angel's visit; she just pondered his sayings in her heart. Therefore, her cousin Elisabeth didn't know what had happened to Mary at the time she began to prophesy. Elisabeth was speaking by the Holy Spirit:

LUKE 1:41-56

41 And it came to pass, that, when Elisabeth heard the salutation of Mary, the babe leaped in her womb; and Elisabeth was filled with the Holy Ghost:

42 And she spake out with a loud voice, and said, Blessed art thou among women, and blessed is the fruit of thy womb.

43 And whence is this to me, that the mother of my Lord should come to me?

44 For, lo, as soon as the voice of thy salutation sounded in mine ears, the babe leaped in my womb for joy.

45 And blessed is she that believed: for there shall be a performance of those things which were told her from the Lord.

46 And Mary said, My soul doth magnify the Lord,

47 And my spirit hath rejoiced in God my Saviour.

48 For he hath regarded the low estate of his handmaiden: for, behold, from henceforth all generations shall call me blessed.

49 For he that is mighty hath done to me great things; and holy is his name.

50 And his mercy is on them that fear him from generation to generation.

51 He hath shewed strength with his arm; he hath scattered the proud in the imagination of their hearts.
52 He hath put down the mighty from their seats, and exalted them of low degree.
53 He hath filled the hungry with good things; and the rich he hath sent empty away.
54 He hath holpen his servant Israel, in remembrance of his mercy;
55 As he spake to our fathers, to Abraham, and to his seed for ever.
56 And Mary abode with her about three months, and returned to her own house.

We can readily see how the word Wonderful applies to the announcement that Jesus was to be born and how He would be conceived.

We'll let the Word of God tell the story of the announcement of His birth as we reminisce on these Scriptures.

LUKE 2:1-20
1 And it came to pass in those days, that there went out a decree from Caesar Augustus, that all the world should be taxed.
2 (And this taxing was first made when Cyrenius

was governor of Syria.)

3   And all went to be taxed, every one into his own city.

4   And Joseph also went up from Galilee, out of the city of Nazareth, into Judaea, unto the city of David, which is called Bethlehem; (because he was of the house and lineage of David:)

5   To be taxed with Mary his espoused wife, being great with child.

6   And so it was, that, while they were there, the days were accomplished that she should be delivered.

7   And she brought forth her firstborn son, and wrapped him in swaddling clothes, and laid him in a manger; because there was no room for them in the inn.

8   And there were in the same country shepherds abiding in the field, keeping watch over their flock by night. [Now notice:]

9   And, lo, the angel of the Lord came upon them, and the glory of the Lord shone round about them: and they were sore afraid.

Not only did the angel appear to them, but it says the glory of the Lord shone 'round about them. That same glory of God was manifested all through the Old Testament: many times as a cloud;

sometimes as a bright, shining light.

10 And the angel said unto them, Fear not: for, behold, I bring you good tidings of great joy, which shall be to all people.

11 For unto you is born this day in the city of David a Saviour, which is Christ the Lord.

12 And this shall be a sign unto you; Ye shall find the babe wrapped in swaddling clothes, lying in a manger.

13 And suddenly there was with the angel a multitude of the heavenly host praising God, and saying,

14 Glory to God in the highest, and on earth peace, good will toward men.

15 And it came to pass, as the angels were gone away from them into heaven, the shepherds said one to another, Let us now go even unto Bethlehem, and see this thing which is come to pass, which the Lord hath made known unto us.

16 And they came with haste, and found Mary, and Joseph, and the babe lying in a manger.

17 And when they had seen it, they made known abroad the saying which was told them concerning this child.

18 And all they that heard it wondered at those things which were told them by the shepherds.

19 But Mary kept all these things, and pondered them in her heart.

20 And the shepherds returned, glorifying and praising God for all the things that they had heard and seen, as it was told unto them.

Chapter 2
WONDERFUL IN MINISTRY

The announcement of Jesus' birth was certainly Wonderful. The 40th verse of Luke 2 shows that He also was Wonderful in childhood:

40 And the child grew, and waxed strong in spirit, filled with wisdom: and the grace of God was upon him.

He was Wonderful in childhood. No wonder His Name should be called Wonderful. Later, He was Wonderful in ministry. When we think about His ministry, we think not only about the healings and the deliverances; we consider all of His ministry. It consisted in *Word* and *works*. Jesus declared in John 14:12, *"Verily, verily, I say unto you, He that believeth on me, the works that I do shall he do also; and greater works than these shall he do; because I go unto my Father.*"

We should carefully study and follow the ministry of Jesus. The Bible says concerning His ministry, "*And Jesus went about all the cities and villages, TEACHING in their synagogues, and PREACHING the gospel of the kingdom, and HEALING every sickness and every disease among the people*" (Matt. 9:35). Our ministry should consist of the same thing.

We also see something about the ministry of Jesus in Luke 4:14, "*And Jesus returned in the power of the Spirit into Galilee: and there went out a fame of him through all the region round about.*" The Bible says He returned in the power of the Spirit. He was Wonderful in ministry.

So we see that Jesus' ministry consisted first of *teaching*, then *preaching*, and, finally, *healing*.

During Jesus' earthly ministry He did

more *teaching* than anything else. You'll discover this if you read through the four Gospels and underline the words "teaching" or "taught." Yet when we think of doing the works of Jesus, we usually think about healing the sick or perhaps casting out devils. Those things are part of it, but teaching also is doing the works of Jesus.

Now notice the 32nd verse: *"And they were astonished at his doctrine: for his word was with power."* Hallelujah!

Then we note the 36th verse of this same chapter: *"And they were all amazed, and spake among themselves, saying, What a word is this! for with authority and power he commanded the unclean spirits, and they come out."* They said that in response to what had happened in the 33rd verse:

LUKE 4:33-37
33 And in the synagogue there was a man, which had

14

a spirit of an unclean devil, and cried out with a loud voice,
34 Saying, Let us alone; what have we to do with thee, thou Jesus of Nazareth? art thou come to destroy us? I know thee who thou art; the Holy One of God.
35 And Jesus rebuked him, saying, Hold thy peace, and come out of him . . . .

In other words, Jesus said, "Shut up!" That's the way you have to deal with the devil — just tell him to shut up. You can't be nice when dealing with the devil.

The rest of verse 35 says: *"And when the devil had thrown him in the midst, he came out of him, and hurt him not."* That devil wanted to act up before he left. He knew it was his last chance, so he threw that fellow in their midst, but he came out and didn't hurt him.

36 And they were all amazed, and spake among themselves, saying, What a word is this! for with authority and power he commandeth the unclean spirits, and they come out.
37 And the fame of him went out into every place of the country round about.

Of course His fame spread. When people get healed and devils are cast out, people talk about it. Jesus was Wonderful: Wonderful in ministry, Wonderful in works, and Wonderful in Words.

Chapter 3
WONDERFUL IN HIS DEATH

Did you ever consider that if it had all ended with Jesus' ministry, there would be no salvation for us? If it had all ended right there, there would be no New Birth.

Thank God, Jesus was Wonderful in His death.

Many people misunderstand when you talk about Jesus' dying spiritually as well as physically. They think "death" means the cessation of life. But *death in the Bible never means cessation of life,* dear friends.

What happened when Adam died spiritually? He still *lived* physically, but he was separated spiritually from God. You see, *spiritual death means separation from God!*

Because Jesus took our place, He had to partake of spiritual death AS WELL AS physical death.

So He cries out here, *"My God, my*

God, why hast thou forsaken me?" You see, God *had* forsaken Him. *That's spiritual death.* He was separated from God. Why did God forsake Him? Because Jesus was made sin for us, and God cannot look upon sin.

Jesus was made sin for us! He took my place! *He became what I was, praise God, that I might become what He is.*

Can you understand that? It's simple — all you have to be is intelligent — yet people want to fight over it. (Actually, when you get down to brass tacks, they believe the same thing, or else they don't believe the Bible — one of the two — or they couldn't be saved.)

Often people will pick some little statement out of context to argue about. Bless their hearts, you feel so sorry for them, but you shouldn't condemn them. You feel sorry for them in the same way you would for a little child who had never gone to school and learned to read. You don't get mad at them because they can't read, and you can't get aggravated with spiritual babies, either. Just have patience with them. Some may grow up someday and become spiritually mature. And if they don't — well, you don't have to worry about it. They've got it made anyway as long as they believe Jesus as their Savior.

"My God, my God, why hast thou forsaken me?" Why did God forsake Jesus? Because He had become sin. Jesus never committed sin. God made Him to be sin with *our* sin. Was it Jesus' body that became sin? No! It was His spirit that became sin, because sin is not a physical thing; it's a spiritual thing. If sin were only physical, then each one of us by dying physically could atone for ourselves. But, no, *sin is spiritual.*

Some of the people standing by the cross, when they heard Jesus say this, said, *"This man calleth for Elias"* (Elijah).

MATTHEW 27:48-51

48 And straightway one of them ran, and took a spunge, and filled it with vinegar, and put it on a reed, and gave him to drink.

49 The rest said, Let be, let us see whether Elias [Elijah] will come to save him.

50 Jesus, when he had cried again with a loud voice, yielded up the ghost [or His spirit].

51 And, behold, the veil of the temple was rent in twain from the top to the bottom, and the earth did quake, and the rocks rent.

He was Wonderful in His death. Hallelujah!

My dear friends, it is very significant that the veil in the Temple was rent in two from top to bottom — very significant. Under the Old Covenant or Old Testament, that veil curtained off the Holy of Holies in the Temple. Flavius Josephus, the Jewish historian, said the curtain was 40 feet wide, 20 feet high, and 4 inches thick.

That means that 20 feet in the air, an angel or similar emissary of God took hold of it and ripped it apart, signifying that the way into the Holy of Holies was now open.

Before Jesus' sacrifice on the cross, no one but the high priest could enter the Holy of Holies, and he had to take great precautions as he entered and made sacrifices for the sins of the people.

The Shekinah glory — the visible presence of God — was kept shut up in the Holy of Holies, but on the day of the Crucifixion, it moved out.

God no longer dwells in an earthmade Holy of Holies; God now dwells in us. The glory of the Shekinah presence of God now dwells in our hearts! The Holy Spirit bears witness with our spirit that we are the children of God.

Chapter 4
WONDERFUL
IN HIS RESURRECTION

Jesus was Wonderful in His death and, thank God, He was resurrected. He was Wonderful in His resurrection. That's part of the Christmas story, too.

MATTHEW 28:1-6

1 In the end of the sabbath, as it began to dawn toward the first day of the week, came Mary Magdalene and the other Mary to see the sepulchre.

2 And, behold, there was a great earthquake: for the angel of the Lord descended from heaven, and came and rolled back the stone from the door, and sat upon it.

3 His countenance was like lightning, and his raiment white as snow:

4 And for fear of him the keepers did shake, and became as dead men.

That means they fell down flat. (You've never seen any dead men standing up, have you?)

5   And the angel answered and said unto the women,
Fear not ye: for I know that ye seek Jesus, which was
crucified.

Are you ready for verse 6? Here's the
Wonderful message, because *"His Name
shall be called Wonderful."*

6   He is not here: for he is risen, as he said. Come,
see the place where the Lord lay.

Where is He? He is not here! All the
powers of earth and hell have failed to keep
Him. According to John's Gospel, Mary
said, *"Sir, if thou have borne him hence,
tell me where thou hast laid him, and I will
take him away"* (John 20:15).

You see, many seek the Living One
among the dead. How many times people
have sought in vain for life among dead
forms. They are seeking life among dead
works, dead feelings, dead services, a dead
god — wells without water.

Everybody else's god in every religion

in the world is dead except ours! He's alive! Thank God, He's risen! He is risen! He is risen! He has all authority!

MATTHEW 28:18
18 And Jesus came and spake unto them, saying, All power is given unto me in heaven and in earth.

That Greek word translated "power" in verse 18 is also translated "authority" throughout the New Testament. Therefore, you could read that verse, "All authority is given unto Me in heaven and in earth."

After His resurrection, Jesus immediately delegated the authority upon the earth to His Church. His authority upon the earth is manifested through the Church.

In the next two verses He sent them forth:

19 Go ye therefore, and teach all nations, baptizing them in the name of the Father, and of the Son, and

of the Holy Ghost:
20 Teaching them to observe all things whatsoever
I have commanded you: and, lo, I am with you alway,
even unto the end of the world.

This is similar to the Great Commission found in Mark's Gospel:

MARK 16:15-18
15 And he said unto them, Go ye into all the world,
and preach the gospel to every creature.
16 He that believeth and is baptized shall be saved;
but he that believeth not shall be damned.
17 And these signs shall follow them that believe; In
my name shall they cast out devils; they shall speak
with new tongues;
18 They shall take up serpents; and if they drink any
deadly thing, it shall not hurt them; they shall lay
hands on the sick, and they shall recover.

There are many thrilling Scriptures along this line, but let's look at the Book of Ephesians, the book with the central theme that Christ is the Head and we are the Body. Let's see the revelation Paul gives in Ephesians. Remember, Paul was not taught the Gospel by some man:

GALATIANS 1:11,12
11 But I certify you, brethren, that the gospel which was preached of me is not after man.
12 For I neither received it of man, neither was I taught it, but by the revelation of Jesus Christ.

The Holy Spirit taught Paul the whole thing! Now notice what Paul says about Jesus' resurrection. He was Wonderful in resurrection.

EPHESIANS 2:1-6
1 And you hath he quickened, who were dead in trespasses and sins;

The word "quickened" means "made alive." Thank God, we've already been resurrected spiritually. We've been made alive. We're going to have new bodies one of these days.

2 Wherein in time past ye walked according to the course of this world, according to the prince of the

power of the air, the spirit that now worketh in the children of disobedience:

3 Among whom also we all had our conversation in times past in the lusts of our flesh, fulfilling the desires of the flesh and of the mind; and were by nature the children of wrath, even as others.

4 But God, who is rich in mercy, for his great love wherewith he loved us,

5 Even when we were dead in sins, hath quickened us together with Christ, (by grace ye are saved;)

God made us alive together with Christ. God saw it as done when He raised Jesus up. Now notice:

6 And hath raised us up together [that's not all of it], and made us sit together in heavenly places in Christ Jesus.

Oh, I could preach on that forever! Yes, He was Wonderful in His resurrection, but that's not all of the story.

Chapter 5
WONDERFUL
IN HIS COMING AGAIN

The birth of Jesus by itself doesn't give us a picture of the complete plan of God. The complete plan of God is not just a little baby lying in a manger at Christmas. If that's all there were to it, it wouldn't be worth remembering. But that wasn't all there was to it. To get a picture of the complete plan of God — Jesus' birth *and* resurrection — let's turn to the first chapter of Acts.

ACTS 1:8-11
8 But ye shall receive power, after that the Holy Ghost is come upon you: and ye shall be witnesses unto me both in Jerusalem, and in all Judaea, and in Samaria, and unto the uttermost part of the earth.
9 And when he had spoken these things, while they beheld, he was TAKEN UP; and a cloud received him out of their sight.
10 And while they looked stedfastly toward heaven as he went up, behold, two men stood by them in white

apparel;

11 Which also said, Ye men of Galilee, why stand ye gazing up into heaven? this same Jesus, which is taken up from you into heaven, shall so come in like manner as ye have seen him go into heaven.

Hallelujah! In conclusion, turn over to First Thessalonians. We must understand something here that many Bible scholars haven't seen, bless their hearts. The result is that many people are trying to peddle little theories of their own.

Remember that Paul said he received the Gospel he preached by revelation of Jesus Christ. *Paul is the only one who received revelation about the catching away of the saints.* (Don't try to read about it anywhere else in the Bible, because you can't.)

We call this "catching away" the "Rapture." If you want to call it "the Rapture," fine; that's scriptural. The event also is called "caught up" (that's what it says in the *King James* translation), or "catching away."

You can't find anyone else in Scripture who has that revelation. When Jesus talked about the Second Coming, He never mentioned the Rapture — and there's a reason He didn't. He was talking primarily to the Jews; He wasn't talking to the Church.

So don't turn over to Matthew 24 and Luke 21 and say, "I read that and there's nothing in there about a Rapture, so one is not going to take place."

Why not? Jesus wasn't preaching or teaching to the Church; He was talking to the Jews. The same disciples who were with Him then were present on the Day of Pentecost. They were endued with power from on High and went out to preach. And we have a double portion of what they preached.

The message spread everywhere they went that Jesus ascended up into heaven, and the cloud received Him out of their sight. Two men in white apparel stood by them and told them, "This same Jesus whom you saw go away is coming in like manner." *He's coming!* The Early Church was looking for Him to come again!

The Church at Thessalonica was looking for Him to come, but in the meantime, some of them had died. Now the others had questions. Were they going to miss it? You can understand why they would be perplexed. Those two men whom the disciples had seen evidently were angels, and they had said, "He's coming."

So now Paul is writing to the Thessalonians:

1 THESSALONIANS 4:13-18

13 But I would not have you to be ignorant, brethren, concerning them which are asleep, [No, their spirit wasn't asleep. Paul is talking about their bodies being asleep.] that ye sorrow not, even as others which have no hope.

14 For if we believe that Jesus died and rose again, EVEN SO THEM ALSO WHICH SLEEP IN JESUS WILL GOD BRING WITH HIM.

15 For this we say unto you by the word of the Lord

[You see, Paul had a Word from the Lord on it.], **that we which are alive and remain unto the coming of the Lord** [Paul is still looking for Him; he expected to be alive and remain, because he used the word "we."] **shall not prevent them which are asleep.**

16 **For the Lord himself shall descend from heaven with a shout, with the voice of the archangel, and with the trump of God: and the dead in Christ shall rise first:**

17 **Then we which are alive and remain shall be CAUGHT UP** [Caught up!] **together with them in the clouds to meet the Lord in the air: and so shall we ever be with the Lord.**

18 **Wherefore comfort one another with these words.**

We read in other places that Jesus is coming back to the earth, but here we see He's coming back *with His saints. How could we COME BACK with Him if we hadn't already GONE to be with Him?*

How could we COME BACK from Oklahoma City if we HAVEN'T BEEN to Oklahoma City?

Yes, Jesus is coming back to the earth eventually, but this is not talking about that here. Can you see that?

CAUGHT UP! We which are alive and remain shall be CAUGHT UP! That's what we mean when we talk about the Rapture — caught up. You may call it either term. There is coming a "catching away." Caught up!

Verse 17 says, *"Then we which are alive and remain shall be caught up TOGETHER WITH THEM in the clouds to meet the Lord in the air: and so shall we ever be with the Lord."* With whom? With those who already have been raised from the dead in Christ.

It says we'll be caught up together with them "in the clouds." We're going to be caught up in the clouds to meet the Lord in the air, and so shall we ever be with the Lord.

He's going to be Wonderful in His Second Coming, isn't He?

Thank God for the Wonderful plan of God — the Wonderful plan of Redemption!